DISCOVERING WASHINGTON WINES

An Introduction to One of the Most Exciting Premium Wine Regions

by Tom Parker

Published by

RACONTEURS PRESS LLC

SEATTLE, WASHINGTON

www.raconteurs.com

Discovering Washington Wines

An Introduction to One of the Most Exciting Wine Regions

by Tom Parker

ISBN 0-9719258-5-2

Library of Congress Control Number 2002092119

Edited by Ann Gosch
Cover by Lanphear Design, Snohomish, WA
Page design and production by Ruth Marcus, Sequim, WA
Indexed by Miriam Bulmer
Cover photographs (other than Mt. Rainier)
   by Douglas Sandberg Photography, San Francisco,
   www.sandbergphotography.com

Copies of this book are available at special discounts when purchased in bulk for premiums and sales promotions as well as for fund-raising or educational use. Special editions or book excerpts can be created to specification.
For details, contact Raconteurs Press LLC at info@raconteurs.com or at:

1426 Harvard Avenue, #443
Seattle, WA 98122-3813 U.S.A.
Tel: 206-329-4688

Table of Contents

Dedicated to the winemakers of Washington
and to those who enjoy the fruits of their harvest.

Introduction

Washington State, long known for its apples and rainy climate, is fast becoming famous for its world-class wines and vineyards. Second only to California in U.S. wine production, Washington produces a much higher percentage of its total volume as higher-quality, premium wines.

The relative speed at which this state has emerged as a major premium wine producer is remarkable. In 1981 there were only nineteen wineries in all of Washington. By 2002 there were more than 170 with new wineries being added at a rate of one every five weeks. The total acreage planted to wine grapes in the state doubles every four years.

Winemaking in this region dates back to the early nineteenth century with the arrival of the first European settlers. Washington's transformation into a major premium wine producer didn't begin in earnest until the 1960s. Much of this transformation, including a giant leap forward in quality, occurred only in the last ten years. The energy among winemakers here reminds many wine industry veterans of California's rise to prominence in the wine world during the 1970s.

Washington wines have an entirely distinctive personality, and many offer great value compared to wines from California and elsewhere. Wine experts and knowledgeable consumers have elevated some to "cult" status. These include several limited-production Bordeaux-style wines offered for sale only to mailing-list customers and exclusive retailers.

The rapid growth of Washington's wine industry has made it difficult to keep up with the number of new premium wine releases and other developments, let alone keep an accurate count of the growing number of wineries in operation. The state currently has five federally recognized wine-producing regions and several unofficial subregions. Wines produced from grapes in each of these areas have their own distinct characteristics and flavor based on unique local growing conditions.

Many winemakers see the future of American wine in the Pacific Northwest. Today Washington is recognized as a major international wine region, but it is still in its early stages of growth compared to other great wine regions around the world. The best is yet to come as future vintages from a growing number of talented winemakers are released.

History of
Washington Winemaking

Wine grapes have been grown in the Pacific Northwest since the arrival of the first European settlers in the area in the early nineteenth century. European explorers had long searched for the Northwest Passage, an all-water route that crossed the western mountains of North America connecting to the Pacific Ocean.

The American sea captain Robert Gray discovered the mouth of the Columbia River in 1792, which he named for his ship "Columbia." Meriwether Lewis and William Clark were the first white explorers to navigate the Columbia River. It was during their expedition of 1804-06 that they traveled west toward the Pacific Ocean through the site of the future Washington State. Although Lewis and Clark didn't find the Northwest Passage, news of their journey soon brought American, British, and French Canadian trappers and traders to the region.

6

The First Wine Grapes

In 1825 the Hudson's Bay Company established a trading post at Fort Vancouver, on the Columbia River across from what is now Portland, Oregon. Early historical records indicate that the first European wine grapes in the Northwest, of the species *Vitis vinifera*, were grown at Fort Vancouver from seeds sent by ship from Europe.

Only grapes from *Vitis vinifera* vines can be used to produce the classic wines refined in Europe over many centuries. Grapes from abundant native American vines did not produce satisfactory results, and early efforts to grow vinifera vines in the eastern United States failed.

Beginning in 1826, *Vitis vinifera* grapes were successfully planted in California. Commercial vineyards were established soon after, marking the beginning of the California wine industry. There are no documented records of wine grapes grown in the Northwest after 1825 until the middle of the nineteenth century.

The Arrival of Railroads and Irrigation

After 1850 the expansion of railroads into the Pacific Northwest brought many immigrants who had seen California's vineyards and recognized the potential for winemaking elsewhere in their new adopted homeland. Italian, French, and other European settlers brought their knowledge of winemaking to eastern Washington and established their own vineyards. Both population and acreage planted to wine grapes expanded rapidly through the end of the nineteenth century. By the 1860s, numerous grape varieties were planted in the Walla Walla Valley.

One notable early vineyard was planted on Stretch Island in Puget Sound by Civil War veteran Lambert Evans in 1872. Evans planted apples and vines of *Vitis labrusca*, a native American grape species that thrived in the wet climate of Puget Sound. Immigration to the region continued to expand after Washington was admitted to the Union in 1889 and received a further boost from the Klondike Gold Rush of 1897 that brought thousands through the state on their way to Alaska, many of whom later settled in Washington.

In 1889 Adam Eckert arrived on Stretch Island from New York State and established a vineyard where he planted a grape called Island Belle. This variety is today known as Campbell Early, which combines *Vitis vinifera* and *Vitis labrusca* vines. Island Belle was widely planted as a table grape and as a juice grape until Prohibition when it became used for home winemaking.

Before 1900, small-scale irrigation began in the arid climate of eastern Washington. Large irrigation projects appeared when railroad companies saw the economic opportunities of projects that enabled them to control water supplies.

In 1903 a subsidiary of the Northern Pacific Railroad created Washington's first large-scale irrigation project at Kennewick. Large commercial farming followed, including plantings of *Vitis vinifera* wine grapes. Kennewick became the center of a thriving grape-growing industry and in 1910 hosted the first Columbia River Valley Grape Carnival featuring entries of more than 40 grape varieties.

Many wineries and vineyards were established in eastern Washington during the years before World War I. Elbert F. Blaine and William B. Bridgman were notable early grape growers in the Yakima Valley who understood the potential for Washington's wine industry. Blaine was a Seattle attorney who managed two early irrigation companies and developed land near Grandview.

Blaine created a farm for himself on one parcel of land and, beginning in 1907, built the Stone House Winery. He was among the first in Washington to hire a professional winemaker, engaging the services of Paul Charvet, who made wines from several grape varieties.

William B. Bridgman was another Seattle attorney who drafted some of Washington's earliest irrigation laws. He began planting table grapes in 1914, followed by wine grapes in 1917. Bridgman helped to create a network of vineyards throughout the Yakima Valley and Columbia Basin by selling vine cuttings to neighbors and friends.

Prohibition

Public sentiment at this time pushed the country toward Prohibition. In 1916 Washington adopted strict anti-alcohol laws that were more stringent than those being considered for national Prohibition. In 1919 Washington ratified the Eighteenth Amendment to the U.S. Constitution, which superseded the state's own prohibition laws.

National Prohibition went into effect on January 16, 1920, but did not completely outlaw alcohol consumption. In fact, home winemakers were allowed to produce up to 200 gallons annually without a permit. For a law that was supposed to eliminate alcohol consumption, 200 gallons seems like a huge loophole and helps explain why demand for wine grapes soared after Prohibition was enacted.

Wineries, however, suffered and many went out of business. Another casualty was the reversal in wine's favorable image among consumers. Before Prohibition, the public had viewed wine as a respectable natural product that belonged at the table as part of a complete dining experience. During Prohibition, however, people's perception of wine changed and it was viewed merely as a source of alcohol and its associated problems.

Part of this change in attitude might be attributed to the disastrous results of home winemakers trying to craft their own brew. This negative perception lingered for many years until after World War II when a more favorable consumer view toward wine emerged.

On December 5, 1933, the U.S. Congress repealed national Prohibition with the Twenty-First Amendment. In that same month, Washington awarded the first bonded license to Charles Somer who created the St. Charles Winery on Stretch Island west of Tacoma.

The repeal of national Prohibition left a void in alcohol legislation across the country. States had to decide what their alcohol policy would be and which laws they wanted to enforce. In 1934 the Washington State Liquor Board was formed. The state legislature passed the "Steele Act" (also known as the Washington State Liquor Act), permitting wine from Washington grapes to be sold directly to taverns and wholesalers.

Wines from out-of-state producers could be sold only through the Washington State Liquor Board and were heavily taxed. This protectionist legislation remained in effect until 1969 and served as a disincentive for Washington winemakers to improve the quality of their product. Cheap, fortified, sweet wines were produced unchanged for many years, shielded from competition by superior wines produced out of state.

Also in 1934, several notable wineries were formed including the National Wine Company (Nawico), Pommerelle Winery, and Upland Winery. These companies would play an important part in the development of the state's modern wine industry.

W. B. Bridgman's Yakima Valley vineyards prospered during Prohibition thanks to strong demand for grapes used in legal home winemaking. He had nearly 200 acres of wine grapes planted when Prohibition was repealed and he opened Upland Winery in 1934.

Bridgman hired Erich Steenborg, the state's only university-educated winemaker. Steenborg was a pioneer in his efforts to create vinifera wines. Upland Winery created some of Washington's first *varietal* wines—wines bearing the name of the principal grape from which they are made—including the state's first dry Riesling. Bridgman and Steenborg set the framework in place for Washington's modern wine industry.

Influence of Dr. Walter J. Clore

Dr. Walter J. Clore is widely regarded as the father of Washington's wine industry for his pioneering research on viticulture in eastern Washington. His work was instrumental in conclusively proving that high-quality vinifera wine grapes could be successfully grown in the Columbia Valley.

Dr. Clore spent more than forty years conducting scientific studies that completely transformed the state's wine industry. Trained as a horticulturist, he began research studies at Washington State College's Irrigation Branch Research Station in Prosser in 1937. There he sought to identify crops suited to the region's many different microclimates. Huge dams under construction at the time would soon provide large-scale irrigation for vast amounts of land that was otherwise too dry to support agriculture.

Dr. Clore experimented with hundreds of varieties of grapes and identified optimal growing sites throughout the Columbia River Valley. His research helped to unlock the potential of eastern Washington's rich volcanic soils and warm climate for vinifera grapes.

In 1951 Lloyd S. Woodburne, a University of Washington psychology professor, joined some friends (including five other University of Washington professors) and started a home winemaking group that began making wine in Woodburne's garage. They believed they could make fine wine from classic European vinifera vines grown in Washington. In 1962 Woodburne's group incorporated as Associated Vintners and planted a vineyard in the Yakima Valley.

In 1967 renowned California wine expert André Tchelistcheff tasted a homemade Gewürztraminer made by Associated Vintners treasurer Philip Church. Tchelistcheff, then wine master at Beaulieu Vineyard in Napa Valley, deemed it the "best in the United States" and after that became an advocate for Washington wines.

In 1954 Nawico and Pommerelle wineries merged to form American Wine Growers (AWG) and began marketing their first varietal wines from grapes grown in eastern Washington. In 1967 AWG hired André Tchelistcheff to help produce its first vinifera wines. The company released its first wines under the Chateau Ste. Michelle label in 1967. Renamed Ste. Michelle Vintners in 1970, the company reorganized in 1986 as Stimson Lane Vineyards and Estates to manage and market Chateau Ste. Michelle and a growing number of winery acquisitions. Today it is the largest winery organization in Washington, producing wines under several brands.

In 1967 Associated Vintners began marketing wines under its own label, later changing its name to Columbia Winery in 1983. In 1979 the company hired David Lake, who became head winemaker and a guiding force in setting new standards for wine quality and innovation.

The Washington Wine and Grape Growers Council funded a project beginning in 1964 at Washington State University that sought to identify the best varieties of grapes for premium wines adaptable for growing conditions in the state. This ten-year project was led by Dr. Clore and marked the first major effort to connect winemakers with grape growers using the Irrigated Research and Extension Center in Prosser. Wine was made from eighty-eight grape varieties out of a total of 149 under evaluation. The project provided solid evidence proving that high-quality wine could be made from vinifera grapes grown in eastern Washington.

California Fights Protectionism

During the 1950s and '60s, California wine producers became increasingly frustrated by protectionist legislation that effectively blocked sales of their wine to Washington consumers. Grape growers and vintners throughout California pressured the California Department of Agriculture to force a boycott of Washington apples if protectionist wine sales restrictions were not removed.

They successfully persuaded the California attorney general to file suit against Washington's regulations in the U.S. Supreme Court, alleging a restraint of trade that violated the guarantee of freedom of commerce under the constitution.

The Supreme Court refused to hear the case, however, and the situation remained unchanged until 1969 when the Washington legislature introduced House Bill 100, a law that would open the state wine market to competition. Supporters of the bill maintained that it would lead the state's wine industry toward improved quality and innovation.

During hearings for House Bill 100, Dr. Clore testified that Washington would be able to "compete very favorably in producing top table and varietal wines with any other region in the United States." His testimony was based on preliminary results from the Wine Project.

Legislators concluded that the state's protectionist laws were the primary reason Washington's winemakers had not made any effort to improve their product, and they voted to enact the bill.

By the 1960s, interest in wine was on the rise across the United States, and many wine enthusiasts began to experiment with home winemaking. Some of these amateur winemakers also began to grow their own wine grapes to supply their small-scale, boutique-winery operations.

After protective tariffs were removed for Washington State wine producers, many marginal wineries went out of business. The remaining wineries were forced to compete with out-of-state vintners by producing better-quality vinifera table wines. In the mid-1970s, only a few Washington wineries were producing premium wines from vinifera grapes, including Chateau Ste. Michelle and Columbia Winery (the latter then known as Associated Vintners). By 1979, only about sixteen wineries in the state were producing about a million gallons of wine annually.

A New Era

The 1970s was a watershed decade for Washington's winemakers as it marked the period when many began to fully recognize the potential for the vineyards of the Columbia Valley and for the state's wine industry.

Dr. George Taylor, president of the Enological Society of the Pacific Northwest, captured the moment best when he said, "Two compelling reasons led to the formation of the Enological Society of the Pacific Northwest (founded in 1973). One was an increasing public interest in all its aspects, from the social to the scientific. The other was the growing realization that we are living in one of the finest grape-growing areas of the country." – Enological Society Newsletter, August 1975.

Recognition of this potential began to spread beyond the state's borders. In 1970 the San Francisco Wine Sampling Club declared

The "French Paradox"

In November 1991 the CBS television program 60 Minutes broadcast a story on the "French Paradox," about an inconsistency between heart disease and lifestyles of French people compared with Americans. Despite less exercise and a similar intake of fat from rich foods, the French have a rate of heart disease only 40 percent of that for Americans.

Washington's wines posed "a serious challenge" to California's best after tasting many Washington State wines.

During the 1970s, several visionary winemakers, often coming from other professions, began producing handcrafted wines that changed people's perceptions of Washington wine. In 1976 Hinzerling Winery was established in the Yakima Valley at Prosser, creating the first "modern" family winery in the state. Preston Wine Cellars (today known as Preston Premium Wines) near Pasco also opened in 1976.

Several other wineries established during this period played pioneering roles. They introduced the boutique winery concept and were the first of a new breed of winemakers to create "Made in Washington" premium vinifera wines. These included Leonetti Cellar in Walla Walla (1977) and Quilceda Creek in Snohomish (1978). Bordeaux-style red wines from both of these wineries set new benchmarks for quality and they continue to do so today. Washington's ascent as a major premium wine producer began in earnest during this decade as the number of wineries and quality of wine increased steadily.

Quilceda Creek Vintners was founded in Snohomish by Alex Golitzen who began making wines in his garage in 1974. Golitzen is the nephew of André Tchelistcheff, the renowned California wine expert who became an influential advocate for Washington wines beginning in the 1960s. Born in France to a Russian émigré family, Alexander Golitzen and his family moved to San Francisco in 1946 to be close to Uncle André who worked at Beaulieu Vineyards in the Napa Valley.

André Tchelistcheff's influence is seen in Alex Golitzen's winemaking style with his judicious use of oak. Quilceda Creek's Cabernet Sauvignon wines are acclaimed for their aromatic yet unobtrusive oak characteristics.

In 1979 David Lake joined the Columbia Winery as enologist and soon became winemaker. He is one of the few winemakers in the state holding the prestigious Master of Wine designation that requires a set of written tests and tastings and is considered to be the most rigorous professional examination in the world of wine. Lake pioneered the introduction of several varietals and was the first winemaker to produce Syrah, Cabernet Franc, and Pinot Gris in Washington.

Lake is known for producing a single-vineyard series of wines and for his experimentation with different varietals new to Washington. Today he is acclaimed for his Columbia Winery Signature series of varietals including Cabernet Sauvignon, Chardonnay, Merlot, Sangiovese, Syrah, and Viognier.

During the 1980s two organizations were established to assist the Washington wine industry: The Washington Wine Institute in 1981 and the Washington Wine Commission in 1983. The Washington Wine Institute lobbies on behalf of its winery members; membership is voluntary. The Washington Wine Commission is a non-

This paradox was explained by the tendency among French people to regularly drink wine with meals, especially red wine. Medical research revealed that moderate alcohol consumption, of red wine in particular, was associated with a lower risk of stroke and heart disease.

The result of the 60 Minutes broadcast was a sharp increase in wine consumption, especially red wine, creating a trend that continues today.

profit trade association with a mission to promote Washington State wines. Commission membership is mandatory (since 1987) for all Washington wineries and grape growers. Both organizations have played guiding roles in helping to develop the state's flourishing wine industry.

The 1980s saw a huge expansion in the number of wineries and vineyards. Thousands of acres of vineyards were planted throughout the Columbia Valley and elsewhere. Numerous wineries were built throughout the Yakima Valley and Walla Walla Valley. By 1990, there were ninety-two wineries in the state producing more than seven million gallons of wine annually.

The trend toward quality accelerated during this decade. In 1989 five Washington wines from different wineries were included in a list of the top 100 wines featured in the December 31 issue of *Wine Spectator* magazine: Hogue Cellars, Johannisberg Riesling; Woodward Canyon Winery, Cabernet Sauvignon; Kiona Vineyards Winery, Chardonnay; Latah Creek Wine Cellars, Merlot; and Columbia Winery, Cabernet Sauvignon.

During the 1990s the number of wineries and vineyard plantings continued to grow, and Washington wines began to win international awards and recognition. At the 1991 Vin Expo in Bordeaux, France, the only gold medal awarded for American red wine was presented to Chateau Ste. Michelle for its 1987 Cabernet Sauvignon. Interest in high-quality wines increased across the United States as tastes toward wine matured and more Americans traveled abroad and were exposed to different cultures.

Winemakers throughout the state began to focus on quality management, which led to widespread adoption of refined winemaking techniques. As a result, the quality of Washington wines took a giant leap forward during the 1990s. Several small artisan wineries released premium reserve Bordeaux-style red wines that attracted widespread international recognition. The November 15, 1994, issue of *Wine Spectator* described Gary Figgins of Leonetti Cellar as the maker of the country's best Merlot and classic Cabernet Sauvignon.

around the forty-sixth and forty-seventh parallels. This northern latitude gives Washington vineyards up to two additional hours of daylight during the peak growing season, compared to California's prime grape-growing regions.

This northerly location also influences fruit characteristics because Washington's ripening month occurs during the last four to six weeks of plant growth. Grapes can be left on the vine longer during the growing season in Washington than they can in California and other more southerly regions. Warm days and cool nights help preserve acid in grapes that provides Washington wines with a distinctive flavor profile.

Winter Freezes

Although Washington has long hours of daylight during the summer, the reverse is true during the winter when daylight hours are very short and temperatures can be very cold. An exceptionally cold winter freeze can damage or kill grape varieties sensitive to cold such as Merlot. Eastern Washington can have drastic changes between daytime and evening temperatures, and in the winter these can be extreme enough to freeze water in grapevines so quickly they will explode.

Killer freezes are a fact of life for Washington's grape growers, who have to plan on losing a significant portion of their crop every five or six years. Historically, this is the frequency for devastating freezes that occur in late January or early February, which can kill vines down to their roots. Freezes in 1991 and 1996 devastated vineyards and sharply curtailed production across eastern Washington.

Growers have learned to mitigate problems associated with freezes through improved site selection and through mechanical means using wind machines when necessary.

Vineyards located close to the Columbia River benefit from its "insulating" effect on air temperature. The water is warmer than the surrounding air in winter, which creates warmer temperatures along the river and helps protect vines from freezing.

Short daylight hours and cold winter temperatures create conditions of very deep dormancy for grape vines, which benefits the following year's crop. Both fruit and vines benefit from improved aromatics if they undergo a deep dormancy.

Pest Protection

Cold winters also seem to have a direct effect on reducing pestilence, particularly phylloxera that has devastated vineyards in California and elsewhere. Phylloxera is a tiny aphid native to North America that feeds on the vine roots and eventually kills the vine.

Native American vines are not susceptible to phylloxera but vinifera and other indigenous European vines are vulnerable. Outbreaks of phylloxera have destroyed vineyards in Europe and California repeatedly since the nineteenth century. The only known successful remedy is to graft vinifera vines on rootstock from native American vines.

Washington is the only major U.S. wine region where vineyards have never been planted using grafted rootstock. Although individual cases of phylloxera have been documented in Washington, no vineyards have had to be destroyed. Cold winters, widely dispersed vineyard locations, and sandy soils are believed to act as natural preventive mechanisms against the pest.

Cold winters are also hoped to prevent the arrival of another potentially devastating pest in Washington that is currently threatening vineyards in California. The glassy-winged sharpshooter (*Homalodisca coagulata*) is a fast-spreading insect that transmits Pierce's Disease while feeding. Pierce's Disease is a lethal, incurable affliction caused by a bacterium that chokes off water and nutrients to grape vines, killing them within a year or two. The glassy-winged sharpshooter is unable to survive prolonged freezing temperatures and should have little chance of survival in Washington's cold winters.

As favorable as Washington's grape-growing conditions are, growers are always vulnerable to periodic severe weather that can sharply reduce the harvest. *Vintage* refers to the grape harvest of a particular year. A look back at data from the last ten vintage years exemplifies how weather ups and downs can affect production of wine grapes.

2001 ▪ 97,600 tons

An excellent vintage from a typical growing season for temperature and vine development. Fruit was harvested at full maturity, and quality appeared to be high for all grape varieties.

2000 ▪ 84,500 tons

This year was marked by a record harvest in almost perfect fruit condition for Washington vineyards. Moderate temperatures throughout the summer and fall helped to maintain grape acid levels, resulting in balanced, fruity wines.

1999 ▪ 65,000 tons

A very cool summer resulted in reduced crop yields. Growers reduced up to 25 percent of existing immature grapes, hoping that vines would redirect energy into a smaller amount of fruit. A warm late summer and fall helped ripen the remaining grapes, maintaining acidity levels and making for lots of wine flavor and intensity.

1998 ▪ 71,000 tons

A cool spell in September delayed the harvest through the end of October. The extended "hang time" enhanced acid levels, resulting in generally high-quality wines.

1997 ∎ 62,000 tons

The growing season was marked by excellent weather conditions and ended with a long, moderate fall, helping to increase acid levels. Overall crop yields were below normal because many vineyards were still recovering from the disastrous winter freeze of 1995-96.

1996 ∎ 34,000 tons

A harsh winter freeze in February followed by a cool growing season destroyed a significant number of vines, sharply reducing yields across the state.

1995 ∎ 62,000 tons

Good weather resulted in a longer than usual growing season, producing a late harvest of very good quality.

1994 ∎ 44,000 tons

An early harvest and reduced crop yields were caused by cool spring weather followed by a hot summer, helping to concentrate flavors.

1993 ∎ 62,000 tons

One of the latest harvests on record for Washington State and an excellent year for white wine varietals.

1992 ∎ 50,000 tons

A mild spring and hot summer helped grapes ripen in the early fall.

1991 ∎ 26,000 tons

A severe winter freeze and a warm harvest season reduced overall crop yields. This was one of the better years for white wines.

The Winemaking Process in Brief

Winemaking can be divided into four basic phases:

Crushing and de-stemming grapes.
Fermenting grapes.
Clarifying and stabilizing the wine.
Ageing the wine.

The juice of nearly all red and white grapes is colorless. The color of red wine comes from contact with grape skins during fermentation. The juice of white wine grapes is fermented by itself.

MAKING WHITE WINE:

1. Grapes are harvested and removed from the stem, and pushed through rollers to release the juice.
2. Grapes are crushed and de-stemmed to create the *must*. The *must* is pumped to a press where the juice is separated from grape skins.
3. The press extracts the juice, which is then cooled and allowed to settle. The grape skins, seeds, and stems are discarded.
4. The juice is "racked" off the residue before being fermented. White wine is made by fermenting the clarified juice, usually in stainless steel tanks. Oak is also used to ferment white wine, especially Chardonnay. Wine may also be cold stabilized during this process.
5. Wine is clarified by racking, fining, and filtration and is then stabilized. Clarification is the process of removing particles, both visible and invisible, that remain in the wine after fermentation.
6. The wine develops a bouquet as it ages, as acids react with fruit, and oxidation changes many ingredients during bulk storage. Once the wine is bottled, no oxygen is available and a different type of development takes place.

MAKING RED WINE:

1. Grapes are harvested and removed from the stem and pushed through rollers to release the juice.
2. Grapes are crushed and de-stemmed to create the *must*. This combination of juice, seeds, and skins is fermented for several days, usually in stainless steel tanks. The *must* is then innoculated with an appropriate strain of yeast or fermented on natural yeasts that exist on the skins.
3. After fermentation, the *must* is pumped to a press where juice is separated from grape skins.
4. Wine is clarified by racking, fining, and filtration and is then stabilized.
5. The wine is aged, in either stainless steel or oak, for anywhere from a few weeks to a few years. The wine is racked and fined several times before bottling. During this bulk storage process, acids react with fruit, and oxidation changes many ingredients. Once the wine is bottled, no oxygen is available and a different type of development takes place. Many red wines will age several years in the bottle before being released.

MAKING SPARKLING WINES

There are several methods used to make sparkling wines. The traditional, and most labor-intensive, process is Méthode Champenoise.

1. A base wine is made in the same manner as a dry white table wine, from grapes with a high acid content and adequate levels of sugar.
2. The wine is bottled, and yeast and sugar are added to generate a secondary fermentation that can take anywhere from six months to many years depending on the style and quality of the resulting wine.

3. During this aging process, bottles are *riddled* (turned continually) and stored in a partially inverted position to allow the *lees* (dead yeast cells) to collect in the neck of the bottle.

4. At the end of fermentation, the neck of the bottle is frozen to solidify the lees, which are removed. Liqueur, brandy, or sweetener called *dosage* can be added at this point, and the bottles are then recorked and wired shut. The wines are then cellared or released for sale.

Another popular method for making sparkling wine is the Transfer Process, which involves less labor through mechanization. The Transfer Process is very similar to process Méthode Champenoise. At the end of the second fermentation, wine is transferred into pressurized tanks where it is filtered before being rebottled.

Removing Corks from Champagne and Sparkling Wine Bottles

Popping sparkling wine corks wastes bubbles and a flying cork can injure someone's eye, break the china, and otherwise wreak havoc while acting as an unguided missile. Sparkling wine bottles should be handled safely and correctly when removing corks.

Make sure that the bottle is properly chilled (around 45 degrees Fahrenheit) and hasn't been shaken. Corks in warm bottles are likely to pop unexpectedly. Carefully remove only enough foil to loosen or remove the twisted-wire hood, while holding the cork with your thumb or hand to prevent it from popping out on its own. Use a towel to wipe off any residue around the cork before opening.

Hold the bottle away from you and anyone else, and tilt it at a 45-degree angle. Hold the cork tightly with one hand, and gently twist the bottle with the other until the cork is almost out of the bottle. The cork should come free of the bottle with a quiet "sigh" rather than a pop. Before pouring, wipe the neck of the bottle with a clean towel or linen.

Bibliography

Asher, Gerald. *Vineyard Tales: Reflections on Wine*. San Francisco: Chronicle Books, 1996.

Clark, Coret. *American Wines of the Northwest*. New York: William Morrow, 1989.

Duncan, Dayton and Ken Burns. *Lewis and Clark: The Journey of the Corps of Discovery*. New York: Alfred A. Knopf, 1997.

Gregutt, Paul, Dan McCarthy, and Jeff Prather. *Northwest Wines*. Seattle: Sasquatch Books, 1996.

Hall, Lisa Shara. *Wines of the Pacific Northwest*. London: Mitchell Beazley, 2001.

Hill, Chuck. *The Gourmet's Guide to Northwest Wines and Wineries*. Seattle: Speed Graphics, 1998.

Irvine, Ron and Walter J. Clore. *The Wine Project: Washington State's Winemaking History*. Vashon, Wash.: Sketch Publications, 1997.

Johnson, Hugh. *Vintage: The History of Wine*. New York: Simon and Schuster, 1989.

Johnson, Hugh and Jancis Robinson. *The World Atlas of Wine*. London: Mitchell Beazley, 2001.

Lukacs, Paul. *The Rise of American Wine*. New York: Houghton Mifflin, 2000.

MacNeil, Karen. *The Wine Bible*. New York: Workman Publishing, 2001.

Peterson-Nedry, Judy and Robert M. Reynolds. *Washington Wine Country*. Portland, Ore.: Graphic Arts Center Publishing Company, 1998.

Pinney, Thomas. *A History of Wine in America: From the Beginnings to Prohibition*. Berkeley: University of California Press, 1989.

Acknowledgments

I am indebted to scores of people throughout Washington who helped me in researching and writing this book, especially the staff of the Washington Wine Commission. Special thanks to the Walla Walla Wine Alliance and to the communications team at Stimson Lane Vineyards and Estates, who went to great lengths in providing resources for research relating to all of Washington's wineries.

I am grateful to those veterans of Washington's wine industry who took time out of their busy schedules to share their experiences and insights including Bob Betz, M.W., of Stimson Lane and Betz Family Winery, Wade Wolfe of Hogue Cellars and Thurston Wolfe Winery, Lorne Jacobson of Hedges Cellars, and Myles Anderson of Walla Walla Vintners and the Walla Walla Community College.

I want to thank those individuals who reviewed my manuscript and shared their insights into the world of Washington wine including Yancy Noll of Esquin Wine Merchants of Seattle, Jennifer Doak, president of the Seattle Chapter of the Wine Brats organization, and Janice Van Cleve, president of the Seattle Chapter of the Enological Society of the Pacific Northwest.

Index

156

About the Author

Tom Parker has been a professional writer and editor for more than twenty years and holds a B.A. degree in history from Kenyon College and an M.B.A. from San Francisco State University. A long-time wine enthusiast, he has followed the story of Washington wines with keen interest in recent years, distilling his observations into this book.

Discovering Washington Wines is the culmination of extensive research on the history of Washington's wine industry and personal interviews with many winemakers and wine professionals across the state.